MARIO LEMIEUX

★

All East End Publishing titles are available at special discounts for sales promotions, premiums, fund-raising, or educational use. For details, write or call: East End Publishing, Ltd., 54 Alexander Dr., Syosset, NY 11791, (516) 364-6383.

MARIO LEMIEUX

★

RICHARD J. BRENNER

EAST END PUBLISHING, LTD.

SYOSSET, NY

To my children, Halle and Jason, with love, and for Anita, who was so helpful. With thanks to Jan Faulkner, Sandy Bogart-Johnton, Heather Rice, Nell Tsacrios and Pat Straughn. Thanks are also due to Craig Campbell at the Hockey Hall of Fame, and Bruce Bernett. But most of all thanks to Nancy Atherton and John Douglas.

MARIO LEMIEUX

ISBN: 0-943403-24-3

First Printing / January 1994

Photo credits: The front cover photo was supplied by ALLSPORT USA. All of the interior photos were supplied by BRUCE BENNETT STUDIOS.

This book is published by East End Publishing, Ltd., 54 Alexander Dr., Syosset, NY 11791.

Mr. Brenner is also available to speak to student groups. For details contact East End Publishing, Ltd., 54 Alexander Drive, Syosset, NY 11791, (516) 364-6383.

Contents

MARIO LEMIEUX

★

1

As Bright as a Diamond

Mario Lemieux was born on October 5, 1965, in Montreal, Quebec, Canada. Mario was the youngest of three boys born to Pierrette, who is a housewife, and Jean-Guy, who is a construction worker.

Mario and his brothers, Richard and Alain, grew up in a small redbrick house in a working class neighborhood of Montreal called Ville Emard. Montreal, the largest city in Canada, is located in the east coast province of Quebec, the only province in Canada in which French, not English, is the official language. And the Lemieux family, like most people in Quebec, learned French in school and spoke French at home. Although Mario picked up bits and pieces of English while he was growing up, and even studied the language while he was playing junior hockey, it wasn't until he began playing for the Penguins and living year-round in Pittsburgh, that Mario became comfortable with his second language.

But when it came to hockey, Mario was fluent from the git-go. Although neither of Mario's parents are athletically inclined, and his brothers were never more than a bit above average when it came to hockey, it was obvious from a very young age that Mario had a special gift for the game.

Mario was taken for his first skating lesson when he was three years old. Like thousands of children before and after him, Mario took his first, tentative steps on the ice while holding onto the arms of a chair, which he pushed forward while he learned to maintain his balance. And like those thousands of other three-year-olds, Mario took his share of flops before he was able to trade in his chair for a hockey stick.

During his first year on the blades, Mario skated under the watchful eye of coach Fernand Fichaud. And even though Mario's parents weren't athletes themselves, they were big hockey fans and attended as many of the practices as they possibly could.

One year after his first hesitant steps onto the rink, when he was still only four years old, Mario showed Fichaud such a spectacular move that two dozen years later the moment still sparkles as bright as a diamond in the memory of the coach.

The play began with Mario taking the puck and skating around two or three defenders. Those moves around his opponents showed nice skating and puck-handling abilities, but by themselves they weren't exactly Play of the Day material. But then Fichaud's jaw fell open in awestruck wonder as Mario skated in alone on the goalie, shifting his body and the puck from side to side until the goalie was pulled completely out of position. Then Mario simply slid the puck into the empty net and raised his stick in glee. Somehow, without ever having been taught the maneuver, Mario had deked out the goaltender. Like the young Mozart, Mario had, untutored, created a thing of beauty at a ridiculously young age. "I think about that move all my life," said Fichaud. "That was the greatest thing I ever saw."

2

Seeing With His Ears

By the time Mario was six years old, he was playing center for the Ville Emard atoms. And even at that age, Mario was a scoring machine who regularly rang up four, five, and even six goals per game.

Mario was a very accurate shooter, and even though he wasn't yet any bigger than the average boy, he had a very hard shot. That lethal combination often caused goaltenders to cringe and tighten up when they saw Mario swooping toward them with his stick raised in the air, ready to drive a stinging slap shot at them. One goalie, Carl Parker, became so intimidated after one of Mario's supersonic shots had hit him in the neck and knocked him to the ice, that the next time Mario came gliding in on goal, Parker just skated out of the crease and allowed Mario to tap the puck into the empty net.

Although he seemed to be able to score almost at will, Mario was never a goal hog. Sometimes, in fact, his coaches would try to get him to shoot more often, but Mario has always seemed to enjoy setting up a teammate as much as he delights in putting the puck in the net himself.

"Mario and I didn't have to shoot from far out," recalled Sylvain Côté, who was a linemate of Mario's for a few seasons at Ville Emard. "We made our play in front of the net. Those 'beauty' goals, you know what I mean? Those tic-tac-toe passes, then bang—in the net."

As Mario grew older, and progressed up the ladder from atom to peewee and then on to bantam, his scoring touch, passing skills, and puck-handling abilities became even more exquisite.

5

One day, while Ville Emard was practicing, Mario started skating in alone toward two retreating defensemen. Suddenly, and without looking, he dropped a perfect pass onto the stick of a trailing winger. The Hurricanes coach was so stunned by what he had just seen that he stopped the practice and asked Mario how he had known where to pass the puck. Mario just shrugged and answered, "I could tell by the sound of his skate blades."

That uncanny ability to make the extraordinary seem ordinary is what elevates the true superstars above everyone else. While most athletes have to learn how to play a sport, and practice each move over and over, like actors rehearsing their lines, there are those few unique individuals who seem to have an inborn genius for the game. Like Albert Einstein in the realm of physics, or Mozart composing sonatas at the age of three, these singular people seem to have an innate ability to grasp and express the inner workings of the game, almost as if their actions were programmed into their DNA.

"If I thought about a move I'd probably turn the ball over," answered Michael Jordan when he was asked if he ever planned the aerial acrobatics that lifted basketball into the realm of ballet. "I just look at a situation while I'm in the air, adjust, create, and let instinct take over."

Great athletes like Mario also have the amazing ability to see pattern in chaos, and to stay so calm that they can process the rapid-fire movements that are going on around them as if they were occurring in slow motion. That's the extra dimension, for example, that allows Joe Montana to stand in the pocket without panicking and scan the field until he picks out an open receiver that other quarterbacks couldn't see. "His concentration, his 'into-it-ness'—it's mind-boggling," gushed George Seifert, the coach of the San Francisco 49ers. "You look at him from the sidelines, and you're almost in awe. You find yourself watching like a fan would."

By the time Mario was six years old, he was the undisputed star of the Ville Emard atoms, having led the Hurricanes to victory in six of the seven intercity tournaments they entered, and skating away with six Most Valuable Player trophies.

As Mario grew older and progressed up to peewee and then on to bantam, his scoring touch, passing skills, and stick-handling abilities became even more developed.

Mario's skills were so startling that word quickly spread beyond the Ville Emard district, and soon hockey fans from all over Montreal were coming to watch the prodigy. He became such a big drawing card that the Hurricanes would pull in thousands of curious fans to a game that would normally attract only a few hundred people.

By the time he was fourteen, Mario had gained a reputation as the best young hockey player in Quebec, and the best prospect that the province had produced since Guy Lafleur had set the minor leagues ablaze in the 1960s, before going on to a Hall of Fame career with the Montreal Canadiens.

3

Always the Best

"I was always the best at the games we played," stated Mario matter-of-factly. "Hockey or baseball, anything physical. As far back as I remember, I was always the best."

That utter belief in himself allowed Mario to play with artistic abandon. Not plagued by the doubts of uncertainty that inhibit minor talents, Mario was free to give full expression to his creative instincts.

That absolute sense of self-confidence is what allows certain individuals to do the unimaginable, as when Michael Jordan seems to defy gravity and walk on air, or when Pablo Picasso, the great painter, kept discovering new ways of seeing and painting the same objects.

That belief in one's abilities creates a core so strong that it allows those individuals to overcome obstacles that would be stopping points for other people. It allows them to see a failure as a temporary setback rather than as a final result. That hardened core is what gave discoverers the courage to venture into the wilderness, or across uncharted oceans. And it also provided the determination that Vincent Van Gogh, the great 19th-century Dutch painter, needed to continue painting despite the fact that he never sold a single one of his works in his lifetime. Now, Van Gogh's impressionistic masterpieces regularly sell for tens of millions of dollars.

And when, for example, Joe Montana was a tenth-string college quarterback in his freshman year at Notre Dame, he never gave up on himself or doubted his abilities. "The key was that I've always believed I could walk onto a football field and make things happen. No matter how many people said I couldn't, I knew I could."

But being that good also made Mario a marked man. Every time he went out on the ice, he would be shadowed by a player whose only role was to skate alongside Mario and try to stop him from scoring. When Mario couldn't be stopped legally, players would foul him, trying to break his concentration or, even better, getting him to retaliate with a cheap shot of his own so that he'd be penalized and sent off the ice. It really didn't matter to the other team if they also had to have a player sitting in the penalty box for a couple of minutes. No one else was as valuable as Mario, so it was always a good tradeoff for the other team.

While Mario wasn't using his head, it's easy enough to understand the frustration of someone who had become a constant target for cheap-shot artists. It's especially hard to turn the other cheek when you're involved in a sport which doesn't do nearly enough to protect its players. Hockey, in fact, is the only sport in which fighting doesn't result in automatic expulsion and suspension.

So while Mario's coaches may have sympathized with his retaliatory actions, they were always trying to persuade him, in one way or another, to stop fighting fire with fire.

Some coaches tried psychology, explaining to Mario that he was allowing his opponents to accomplish their aim of taking him off the ice, where he ruled supreme, and putting him in the sin bin, where he was just another hockey goon.

One coach would make Mario write one hundred times: *I must not get misconduct penalties.* Another coach made the mistake of screaming at Mario after a game: "Four penalties. Stupid!" Mario grabbed the score sheet out of the hands of his irate coach and smugly said, "Seven points for me, tonight. That's not so bad."

Mario has never been one to accept being yelled at. "One thing I've always hated is people screaming at me. If you want me to do something, talk to me. When someone screams at me to hurry up, I slow down."

The only tactic that seemed to have any effect upon Mario was when one of his coaches would bench him. The benching would usually produce a tearful apology from Mario, but it also, invariably, put the Hurricanes on the short side of the scoreboard. In one game, against the Montreal North, Ville Emard fell behind by a 6–1 score while Mario sat out the entire second period, watching the thrashing through teary eyes.

Although the game seemed hopelessly out of reach, Mario begged his coach to let him play the final period. Then he went out and put on a super spectacular six-goal performance that lifted the Hurricanes to an improbable 7–6 win.

Challenging situations have always seemed to stoke Mario's competitive fires. On or off the ice Mario has always been a fierce competitor and a bad loser. Whether he was playing hockey or a family game of Monopoly, the Lemieux knew that they would have to brace for a stormy tantrum if Mario wasn't the winner. "If Mario lost," recalled his father, "it would be as if a hurricane went through the basement."

In most social situations, though, the hurricane turns into a whisper, with Mario preferring to stay in the background. Outside of his family and a close circle of friends, Mario has always been very self-contained. As one old friend from their days in Ville Emard remembered, "When he was with two or three close friends, there was lots of jokes. But when someone else came by who he didn't know so well, he was always quiet."

Mario has always been quiet in the locker room, as well. Although he was always the star on the teams that he played for, he never lorded his celebrity over his teammates. When he left the rink, Mario always tried to step out of the limelight.

4

A Mixed Bag

Nineteen-eighty-one turned out to be a big year in Mario's young life. With 62 goals in only 40 games, he was the league's top gun while playing for the Montreal Concordia team in Midget Triple A hockey.

That showing secured his selection by Laval, who owned the number-one overall draft pick in the Quebec Major Junior Hockey League. It also caused hockey agents to come knocking at the door of the Lemieux's redbrick home. Mario, who was still only fifteen years old, decided to sign with Bob Perno, who had a close relationship with Wayne Gretzky. The Great One, who had just topped off his third year with the Edmonton Oilers by setting a new NHL scoring record, was idolized in Canada as the best hockey player in the world.

Although the Gretzky connection had given Perno an opening with Mario, the agent sealed the deal by promising to get Mario a million-dollar NHL contract if Mario delivered on his boast to break the Quebec junior scoring records and become the best junior player on the planet.

During that summer of 1981, Perno introduced Mario to a new game—golf. It was love at first swing for Mario, who has gone on to become an avid and accomplished golfer. He has become so good, in fact, that sometimes he talks about playing the sport on a professional basis after he retires from hockey.

"I would like to play golf professionally when I'm finished with hockey. That is my dream, anyway. There is something clean and bright about golf. It's a game where you are alone

13

and within yourself. That's something I like sometimes, to be alone and to see what is inside myself.

"Sometimes with hockey—although I try not to let it be so —there is no time for reflection. Thinking is important. Thinking what you are."

It was during that summer that Perno introduced Mario to Wayne Gretzky. Gretzky, who was almost five years older than Mario and an NHL All-Star, graciously took the time to befriend Mario, a fifteen-year-old who hadn't even played his first game of junior hockey. The meeting took place in Toronto, on a day when Gretzky was taping a television commercial. Instead of politely dusting off the starstruck youngster, Gretzky allowed Mario to tag along and watch the making of the commercial. Then Gretzky topped off the day by taking Mario out to dinner.

Mario was so taken by the Great One that he decided to change his uniform number. Instead of continuing to wear the number 27, which he had always worn, he would start his career in juniors by wearing the number 99, which Gretzky had made famous. Perno, though, was able to convince Mario that 99 had become the Great One's signature, and that Mario should carve out his own unique identity. As an alternative, Perno suggested that Mario could wear the number 66, which was 99 turned upside down. It was an idea that met with immediate acceptance.

Mario's first season with Laval turned into a mixed bag. Although he wound up pacing all first-year players by scoring 96 points in 60 games, he didn't produce the spectacular performances that were expected from him, and he was beaten out for Rookie of the Year honors.

Mario had gone to the awards banquet with his family and Bob Perno, firmly believing that he would be toting the trophy home. When the bad news was announced, Mario reacted bitterly. "I know I'm a better player," he told Perno.

"I'll show them. I'm going to become the best player in the world."

Mario picked up his pace dramatically in his second season in juniors, as he scored 184 points, including 84 goals in only 66 games. Mario's scoring exploits also led Laval to a first place finish, but he still wound up playing second fiddle, this time to Pat LaFontaine. The speedy LaFontaine, who has gone on to have a star-studded NHL career with the New York Islanders and the Buffalo Sabres, topped Mario's output with a league-high 224 points.

But it wasn't only in the scoring race that Mario trailed LaFontaine. The American-born skater was actually more popular with the people of Quebec than Mario, the hometown star who was born in the province. The fans loved LaFontaine's quicksilver game, which was built on speed and motion. He reminded them of the glory years of the Montreal Canadiens, when their high-speed skaters earned the team the nickname, the Flying Frenchmen, and Stanley Cup championship celebrations seemed to be an annual birthright of the people of Quebec.

And while Mario is not a slow skater, his game relies on anticipation rather than speed. He will, more often than not, wait for the puck to come to him rather than chase it around the rink. And with his large wing span, Mario is often able to reach out and gather in a puck that other players have to skate to.

But the difference between the two skaters was even more than a question of points or style. LaFontaine played the game with a puckish enthusiasm and an obvious delight, whereas Mario seemed to approach the game with an almost businesslike attitude and with a deadpan expression on his face. As Marc Lachapelle, a Montreal hockey writer, put it, "He played the game and he came to the rink to practice. That was his task. And that was it."

And whereas LaFontaine was a high-energy performer

who played hockey with a nonstop, all-out effort, Mario sometimes seemed to cruise through patches of a game as if he were a spectator on the ice. "Mario was there, but you didn't see him," said Yves Courteau, a Laval teammate. "And when he didn't have the puck, he was just an average player," added Courteau, which suggested that Mario wouldn't dig for a puck, or play an active role on defense.

Mario didn't bother to deny his lack of effort on defense, telling Bob Perno, "I've got the puck about seventy-five percent of the time I'm out there. That's not such bad defense."

Mario thought that he was overly criticized and under-appreciated. "It's not easy when you're bigger than others. They say I'm overloaded with talent. But they forget that I work as much if not more than the others to polish my game, to be at the top of it, to get the results that everyone expects of me."

But the critical comments were justified. Exquisite offensive skills don't justify a lack of determination on defense. And the fact of the matter is that Mario didn't always go all out. Sometimes he seemed to flip an imaginary switch and play for stretches as if he were skating on cruise control.

Some people attributed those lapses to the fact that Mario was so much more talented than the other players that the games weren't consistently challenging enough for him. Other critics claimed that Mario was moody, having been spoiled by overindulgent parents, and that he played hard only when he chose to.

While there was some truth in all of the above, there was also the plain fact that Mario, for whatever the reason, had a lazy streak. He had the desire to be the best, but he didn't, as yet, have the determination to work consistently and steadily toward his goal.

When he was playing for Ville Emard, that lack of discipline hadn't handicapped Mario, because his natural abilities had been so much greater than those of the people he had played against.

He had been born with exceptional eye-hand coordination, and he possessed an innate sense of the game that defied teaching. He also had an accurate, powerful shot, and the skill to consistently thread a pass through a maze of moving sticks and bodies. And by the time he was sixteen years old, Mario had grown to 6' 4" and filled out to 200 pounds. So even though he shunned the weight room, he was stronger than most of the players he skated against.

Mario had all of the tools that he needed to be the best player, but he was lacking the discipline to work and develop the full tapestry of his unique talents. He had all of the hardware, but he was missing the inner fire that propelled Pat LaFontaine to the scoring title and that fueled Wayne Gretzky into becoming not only the greatest player in hockey but, even more importantly, the best hockey player that Wayne Gretzky could possibly be.

5

Player of the Year

As Mario approached his third and final season with Laval, he realized that this was his last chance to fulfill the boast he had made to Bob Perno three years earlier: to break the Quebec Major Junior League scoring records and become the best junior player in the world.

Toward those ends, Mario worked out during the summer and came to training camp with a new and improved attitude. He was determined, now, to break the single-season record of 130 goals that had been set by Guy Lafleur during the 1971–72 campaign, and the total points mark of 251 that had been established by Pierre Larouche during the 1973–74 season.

Mario started chasing the records as soon as the first puck of the 1983–84 season was dropped. Mario was such a steady and relentless pursuer that he scored at least one point in the first 61 games of the season, shattering the single-season consecutive game scoring streak of 43 that LaFontaine had set the prior year, and the 60-game streak that Lafleur had established over a two-season span.

By the end of his 66th game, Mario already had Larouche's total points mark in his back pocket. But with only four games left in the season, he had "only" 118 goals, a dozen less than Lafleur had registered in a 62-game schedule. And even after Mario had picked up his pace by scoring nine goals in his next three games, he still needed another hat trick in the season finale, just to tie Lafleur's record.

Apparently undaunted by the prospect of playing what he at the time called, "the biggest match I will play since I have put on skates," Mario went out in front of a packed arena

19

that included Wayne Gretzky, and electrified the crowd with a *double* hat trick that boosted his final total to 133. Mario also picked up five assists to compile an 11-point night and finish out the season with 282 points.

Gretzky, who had watched the game with his Edmonton Oilers teammate, Paul Coffey, had seen the future. "This is the guy who is going to take my place," said the always-gracious Great One.

Mario was thrilled by his accomplishments, and jealous of the records he had worked so hard to achieve. "I don't want my records broken," said Mario, who was unwilling to express the usual palaver that records are meant to be broken.

Mario's final year at Laval was marred somewhat, however, by a controversy in the middle of the season, and a disappointing postseason showing in the Memorial Cup, the tournament that brings together the best Canadian junior hockey teams.

The controversy stemmed from Mario's refusal to join the Canadian team of all-stars that was selected to go to Sweden and compete for the world junior championship. Mario, who had had an unhappy experience in an international tournament the previous year, refused to go. His official reason for refusing to play was that he wanted to be at home with his family during the Christmas holiday. The unofficial reason was that he didn't want to take any time off from his record-chasing run at Lafleur and Larouche.

The powers-that-be in the Quebec Junior Hockey League were outraged by Mario's stand, and instead of simply naming a substitute they tried to force his hand by enacting a resolution to suspend any player who refused to play for Team Canada.

Mario, still refusing to capitulate, even though newspaper columnists were publicly denouncing him as being ungrateful and unpatriotic, took the league to court to prevent the suspension from taking effect. The judge who heard the case ruled in Mario's favor, sustaining the point that Mario wasn't under any legal obligation to play for Team Canada. Mario took a lot of heat for standing up to the hockey establishment, so it was a real testament to his inner strength that he could put the nasty affair aside, and continue on his record-setting rampage.

Mario continued to rewrite the record book in the Quebec league playoffs, where in 14 games he set new standards for goals (29), assists (23), and total points (52), while leading Laval to the provincial title. Mario's playing season, however, came to a surprisingly sour ending. He could score only two points while Laval was suffering three straight losses and being swept out of the Memorial Cup tournament.

Mario was disappointed in not being able to lead Laval to the Memorial Cup championship, and deliver on a promise he had made to the team's owner. But Mario did make good on his promises to Bob Perno. He had broken the Quebec junior scoring records, and when the votes were tallied, Mario was named the 1983–84 Canadian Major Junior Player of the Year.

Mario scans the ice.

It's not all goals and glory.

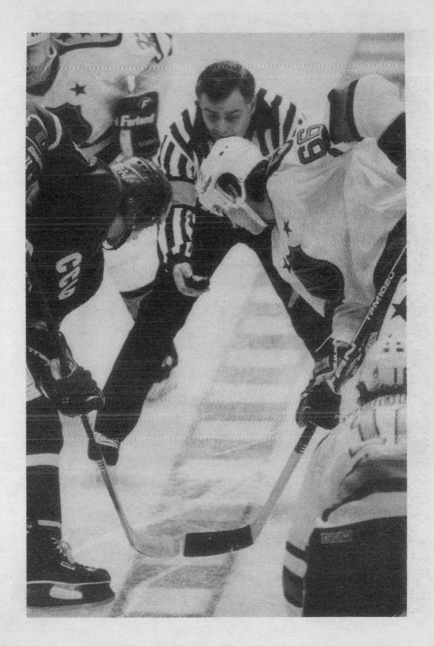

Mario facing off at the 1987 Canada Cup.

All-Stars Brett Hull and Mario.

Tom Barrasso and Mario share a smile and the 1991 Stanley Cup.

The long reach of Mario.

Mario facing off against Wayne Gretzky.

Just as sweet the second time around.

Mario and some teammates celebrating their 1992 Stanley Cup win.

Mario collecting some hardware in 1993.

6

Rookie of the Year

The Pittsburgh Penguins owned the rights to the top pick in the 1984 draft by virtue of finishing at the bottom of the NHL standings with a 16–58–6 record.

Most years, there isn't a noticeable talent differential among the most highly rated junior players, and any of a half dozen or so could wind up as the number-one pick. But every now and again, a Gretzky or an Eric Lindros just pops right up to the top of the draft. Nineteen-eighty-four was one of those now-and-again years, with everyone who followed hockey realizing that Mario was a franchise player, a talent that you could build a team around—even a team as pathetic as the Pittsburgh Penguins.

The Penguins general manager at the time, Eddie Johnston, had Mario already measured for a Pittsburgh sweater. The only problem was, Mario wasn't willing to put it on.

On the day of the draft it is traditional for the players who are picked to go over to the table of the team that has selected them, put on the team's sweater, smile, and say *cheese* for the newspaper photographers. Mario, however, wasn't willing to go along with the tradition unless a contract could be worked out prior to the draft. Acting under the instructions of then-owner Edward DeBartolo, the Penguins had topped out at $760,000 spread over three years, but Mario was holding out for an even million dollars, the number that Perno had promised to get for Mario three years earlier.

The draft took place at the Montreal Forum, the high temple of hockey arenas. And for the first time, the draft proceedings were going to be televised throughout Canada and into Pittsburgh. The pressure on Mario was intense.

When his name was called, Mario, sitting with his family and Bob Perno, got up and waved, but he stood fast and refused to go down to the Penguins' table.

Once again Mario had clashed with the hockey establishment, and once again most of the public and the press had sided with the power brokers. One Canadian reporter went so far as to call Mario's action, "A tasteless demonstration of bad manners, unmatched by anything I've ever seen."

What these people didn't stop to realize, apparently, was that hockey was—and still is, to a large extent—a game controlled by willful and paternalistic owners who were used to treating their players as pawns, drafting them, trading them, and paying them as the owners, and only the owners, saw fit. The owners in effect had always acted as strict parents, while the players were expected to behave like obedient children.

Instead of seeing Edward DeBartolo, who was a billionaire and one of the richest men in North America, as a tightwad who was trying to play hardball against a teenager who had very little leverage—it wasn't as if Mario were free to sign with some other team—the public and the press depicted Mario as an arrogant and spoiled brat.

Within a week of the draft-day controversy, the two sides got together and agreed to a three-year contract that would allow Mario to earn his million dollars, if he scored a specified number of goals and points.

With the contract squabbles out of the way, Mario arrived in Pittsburgh, only eighteen years old and about to be living away from home for the first time in his life—away from his close-knit family and his steady girlfriend, Nathalie Asselin, and away from the French-Canadian culture in which he had been raised. Although Mario had started taking English lessons while playing for Laval, he still wasn't fluent in the language, or comfortable when speaking it, especially to strangers. "There were times when reporters would ask me questions," recalled Mario, "and I would only answer, 'yes,' 'no,' or 'I think so,' because I wasn't quite sure of the question."

The Penguins general manager, Eddie Johnston, came up with a smart way to help Mario ease into his new situation. He arranged for Mario to live in the suburban home of Tom and Nancy Matthews and their three children. Living with the Matthews would not only make it easier for Mario to learn to speak English, but it would also guarantee that he was eating well, keeping regular hours, and having the family-type setting to which he was accustomed. And with all the little details taken care of, Mario would be free to concentrate on hockey.

Although Johnston had taken care of Mario's living arrangements, he hadn't done much in the way of providing him with capable teammates. But Mario appeared to be unconcerned with the fact that the Pens, losers in thirteen of their seventeen NHL seasons, were coming off the very worst record in their sad-sack history.

In his three seasons with Laval, Mario had helped turn a last-place team into a first-place one, so he wasn't about to be cowed by the Pens' past failures. "I like to play with a team that is very low, and get the team up in a few years," said Mario in his faltering English.

Opening night in the NHL for Mario was October 11, 1984, and he broke into the big leagues with a bang, by beating Bruins goalie Pete Peeters with the first shot he ever took as an NHL player.

With just over a minute and a half gone in the game, Mario went over the boards at the Boston Garden, and on the first shift of his NHL career intercepted a pass by Boston's All-Star defenseman, Ray Bourque. Mario poked the puck ahead, faked a shot with his forehand that pulled Peeters to his knees, and then calmly lifted a backhand shot into the back of the net. Mario later added an assist, but it wasn't enough, naturally, to keep the Pens from losing the game,

35

4–3. Mario also picked up a point on his first shift in front of the hometown fans in Pittsburgh's Civic Arena, more familiarly known as the Igloo.

Another early-season highlight occurred when the Edmonton Oilers came to town, producing the first on-ice meeting between Mario and Wayne Gretzky. While Mario picked up a point on an assist, Gretzky came up bigger by scoring a late-game goal that enabled the Oilers to slide away with a 3–3 tie.

Although reporters were already trying to stir up a rivalry between 66 and 99, Mario knew that he wasn't yet ready to challenge the Great One. "It isn't very fair to compare me to Wayne Gretzky. He's the greatest. I'll try to be the best, but it will take me more than a handful of games to do that."

It took a while for Mario just to settle in to the NHL and start to feel comfortable. "The first ten games were really tough because I felt a lot of pressure to do well," said Mario, who was held to only one goal in his first eleven games. "The pace of play is so much faster, the players are bigger, stronger, and smarter, and if you make a mistake, they take advantage of it."

Eventually, though, Mario got into the flow of the game and began to pile up the points. He realized he could play his game, but at this level he just had to play it a lot smarter and faster. "After maybe thirty games I really started to play well, started to control games a little more."

Mario did so well, in fact, that Al Arbour, the New York Islanders coach, added Mario to the 1985 Wales Conference All-Star team. Mario rewarded Arbour's faith in him, and showed that he deserved his spot on the squad, by scoring two goals and an assist while skating off with the All-Star Game MVP award. "Winning that MVP award in Calgary really made him feel he belonged," recalled Eddie Johnston. "From then on, he took off."

Mario, who finished his initial season in the NHL with 43

goals and 57 assists for an even 100 points, the third highest total for a rookie in league history, added to his hardware collection by taking home the Calder Trophy as the NHL's Rookie of the Year.

In addition to putting points up on the scoreboard, Mario had also brought bodies into the Igloo, raising the Penguins' average attendence from 6,800 the previous year to 10,000. But there was still a lot of work to be done, both in terms of filling the Igloo, which can hold over 16,000 people, and in sealing up the weak spots in Mario's game.

Even though he had cracked the century mark, the fact was that opposing teams had lit the red light 135 times while Mario was on the ice, which gave him a −35 rating. And while the Pens had managed to improve their win total from 16 to 24, they were still the tailenders of the Patrick Division and a lot of long strides away from becoming a playoff contender.

All things considered, though, it had been a very successful year, and Mario was ready for a long rest. But instead of heading for a golf course, he agreed to play for Canada in the World Hockey Championships, which were being staged in Prague, the capital of the former Czechoslovakia.

Although he went to Prague reluctantly, Mario left the city all-aglow after he had scored two goals and led the Canadian team to a 3–1 upset and the silver medal over a team from the former Soviet Union. "It's not every day you get a chance to beat the Russians," beamed Mario. "Doing this is a greater thrill than I ever dreamed of."

7

Holding Pattern

Prior to the start of Mario's sophomore season, Ed Johnston made some minor moves to improve the team. But it was obvious to anyone who even glanced at the Pens' still-shallow talent pool that any upward movement in the standings would have to be powered by the nineteen-year-old kid who wore the number 66 on his broad back.

Mario did his part and more for most of the season, scoring at least one point in 65 of the 79 games in which he played, including a 28-game scoring streak in which he racked up 59 points.

Although he had built his game on finesse, at 6' 4" and filled out to 210 pounds, Mario now had the strength to overpower people as well as the ability to go around them. As veteran coach Mike Keenan pointed out, "Mario's size gives his game a whole different dimension. He's learned how to beat you with his size. That's why he's so effective around the net."

And with his long reach, Mario was able to use his stick the way a great matador uses his cape, teasing a defender into reaching for the puck and then, when the player had committed himself and was off balance and out of postition, pulling the puck back. With the defender rendered totally defenseless, Mario would either swoop in on the goalie or snap a laserlike pass to a winger moving toward the net.

But Mario stumbled in the home stretch, causing the Penguins to waddle to the finish line with 12 losses in their final 16 games. That was just enough losing to knock them out of the playoff picture. Although the Pens had taken a giant step forward by winning 34 games, 10 more than they had the previous season, they were still on the outside looking in at postseason play.

His late-season slump notwithstanding, Mario still piled up 141 points to finish as the long-distance runner-up to Wayne Gretzky, who set a single-season NHL scoring record by tallying 215 points. After two seasons of NHL play, Mario had registered 241 points which, by a strange coincidence, was the exact number of points that Gretzky had recorded in *his* first two seasons with the Edmonton Oilers.

Mario finished second to Gretzky in the voting for the Hart Trophy, which is given to the NHL's MVP. But Super Mario did win the Lester B. Pearson Award, which is given to the best player in the league, as voted on by the National Hockey League Players Association, whereas the Hart Trophy is voted for by the media.

Mario's standout sophomore season earned him a new contract and a hefty raise, which made him the second highest paid player in the NHL, behind—you guessed it—Wayne Gretzky.

Mario began the 1986–87 season with a scoring surge that hot-wired the Pens to a 7–0 start and earned him NHL Player of the Month for October.

Although both Mario and the Pens cooled down as the season wore on, as long as their Main Man remained in the lineup, the Pens playoff hopes were at least lukewarm. But when Mario was sidelined for thirteen games with a knee injury, the talent-thin Pens went into a deep freeze in which they won only two games.

Even after he returned to the lineup, Mario didn't turn on the juice often enough to propel the Pens into the playoffs. What made matters even more bleak was that, after two seasons of steady improvement, the Pens slipped, winning only thirty games and once again finishing in fifth place in the Patrick Division, just one step above the basement.

Mario also showed some slippage, both in his performance

and on the public relations front. Although he finished third in the league in scoring (107) and in goals (53), his points-per-game were down from the prior year; and for the first time in his three years in the Steel City, some of the Pittsburgh reporters who covered the Penguins began to express impatience with Mario's sometimes lackadaisical play. They chided Mario to bring his work ethic up to the level of his talent. "If not," said one scribe, "Mario will always be a pale copy of Wayne Gretzky, and the Penguins will remain mired in mediocrity."

Mario was ready for a long vacation, so he declined an offer to play in the 1987 World Championships. Although Mario had had a good experience at the 1986 tournament, he decided it was time to put away his hockey sticks and pick up his golf clubs. His rejection of the offer to play for the Canadian team once again provoked the ire of the hockey establishment.

It was ironic that a season which had started so sweetly had ended on such a sour note.

8
Lift-off

Just when it appeared that his NHL career might be in an holding pattern, Mario launched it into a superstar orbit with a season-long display of hockey brilliance.

Mario lit the fuse for the lift-off at the 1987 Canada Cup, a preseason tournament that featured the national teams of Canada and the United States as well as the top European hockey powers. Playing with and against the greatest array of hockey stars in the world inspired Mario to intensify his effort and to lift the level of his game to new heights.

While Mario played exceptional hockey throughout the entire tournament, as the games increased in importance his play became even more extraordinary. When, for example, Team Canada needed a win to reach the three-game final series against the USSR, it was a two-goal, three-point effort by Mario that sparked them to a 5–3 triumph over the Czechoslovakian team.

Although Mario posted two assists in Game One of the Canada Cup finals, that wasn't enough firepower to prevent the Soviet squad from skating away with a thrilling 6–5 overtime win.

For most of the preceeding games in the tournament the Team Canada coach, Mike Keenan, had played Mario and Wayne Gretzky on separate lines, thinking that it was wasteful to have his two best centers on the ice at the same time, and sharing one puck. But after the opening game loss, Keenan decided to pair his two superstars. All at once it seemed as if the ice had been sprinkled with magic crystals.

With Gretzky acting as the quarterback, Mario racked up the final three goals, including the overtime winner that reversed the 6–5 loss in the first game and evened the series at 1–1. The Dynamic Duo also teamed up in the decisive third game as Mario converted a Gretzky pass into the goal that lifted Team Canada to another 6–5 win and the Canada Cup championship.

Mario, who set an all-time Canada Cup record with 11 goals, had finally been given the opportunity to express the full range of his exquisite abilities, and he had responded by shining as brightly as the brightest star.

Mario left the Canada Cup tournament with a renewed admiration for the artistry and intensity with which Wayne Gretzky, his MVP-winning teammate, played the game of hockey. "Every shift, Wayne tried to do the impossible." Realizing that he could play at Gretzky's level if he played with the same intensity was an important step in Mario's development. "He gave me a lot of confidence in myself, and I brought it back to Pittsburgh."

When Mario caught up to the Penguins in training camp, he was appointed team captain by new coach Pierre Creamer, and also given the added role of being a penalty killer. Creamer thought that killing penalties would make Mario a stronger two-way player by forcing him to concentrate on defense. Creamer also knew that opponents would have to slow down their power plays or risk losing the puck, creating the scary scenario of Mario skating in solo on their goaltender.

One goalie made Mario on a breakaway seem like the hockey version of the Prince of Darkness. "As soon as he gets the puck, you think to yourself, 'It's him, he's got it and he's going to get ya,'" said Hartford Whalers netminder Sean Burke. "This big, menacing figure is on you before you know it, and then you have only a split second to try to make the play."

In that situation, though, it's usually Mario who is going to make the play. As veteran goalie and former teammate Wendell Young noted with a laugh: "Most of the time when you see him coming, you might as well bend over and kiss your butt good-bye."

Although Creamer would wind up getting axed after the season, his strategy of putting Mario on the penalty-killing unit worked out perfectly, with Mario banging home 10 shorthanded goals, to lead all NHL scorers.

General manager Eddie Johnston also added to the Pens' striking power with a November trade with the Edmonton Oilers that put All-Star Paul Coffey, a two-time winner of the Norris Trophy as the NHL's top defenseman, in a Pittsburgh uniform. Mario, who had played with Coffey in the Canada Cup, was delighted with the swap. "A guy like Coff opens up the ice so much for the other guys," smiled Mario as he licked his lips and thought about Coffey's skating speed, stick-handling, passing, and scoring abilities. With the addition of Coffey, who two seasons earlier had set the single-season record of goals by a defenseman with 48, the Pens had created one of the most potent even-strength and power play combos in the NHL.

With Coffey and Mario on the ice at the same time, opponents would now be forced to divide their attention between two high-scoring superstars, creating momentary pockets of indecision that would multiply the Pens' scoring chances.

Mario exploited so many of those opportunities that he was snapping at Gretzky's heels in the race for the Art Ross Trophy as the league's top point producer. And when Gretzky missed several weeks with a knee injury, Mario surged into the lead.

The 1988 All-Star Game, played in St. Louis, gave Mario another stage on which to parade his magnificence, and he didn't disappoint. In a performance that ranks with the very best in All-Star Game history, Mario had a stick in each of the six goals that the Wales Conference scored. Dividing his energies evenly between playmaking and putting the puck in the net, Mario assisted on three goals and scored the other three himself, including the overtime tie-breaker that sunk the Campbell Conference 6–5 and earned Mario the MVP award. "That was a scary performance," said Mike Keenan, who coached the Wales Conference All-Stars. "I'd like to congratulate the rest of the team, but Mario was just awesome tonight."

Mario also finished the regular season in spectacular style by capturing the Art Ross Trophy as the NHL's top point producer, snapping Gretzky's streak of seven straight scoring titles. And then Mario, who had racked up a league-high 70 goals, capped his big breakthrough season by winning the Hart Trophy as the NHL's MVP, ending the glittering reign of Gretzky who had, astonishingly, won the award for eight consecutive seasons.

At only twenty-two years of age, Super Mario had become, behind Gretzky and Hall of Fame defenseman Bobby Orr, the third youngest player to win the Hart Trophy, and the second youngest, after Orr, to snare the Hart and Art Ross Trophies in the same season.

Mario's play had also helped get the Penguins back on the right track. Although they had finished at the bottom of the Patrick Division, they had missed the playoffs by only one point, and had finished merely seven points behind the division-winning New York Islanders. Moreover, the Pens had wound up with a 36–35–9 record, the first time in nine seasons that they had managed to finish above the .500 level. So, while there was still some ground to cover, with Mario leading the way, the Pens were at least pointed in the right direction.

Some people saw the 1987–88 season as a changing of the guard, with Mario replacing Gretzky as the NHL's premier player. But Gretzky's defenders were quick to point out that he had played thirteen fewer games than Mario, and that his points-per-game average was actually slightly higher than

Mario's (2.32 to 2.18). And the people who had watched Gretzky work his magic for ten seasons weren't about to desert the Magician so quickly. "Wayne has proved himself every year," noted Bobby Clarke, a former NHL All-Star center who is currently a hockey executive. "Mario has mountains to climb before he can be called as good as Wayne."

Still other supporters of Gretzky pointed out that he had guided the Edmonton Oilers to four Stanley Cup championships, whereas Mario, in his four NHL seasons, hadn't even been able to propel the Penguins into the playoffs. It was the same argument that was going on among basketball fans, many of whom were claiming that, while Michael Jordan might have great talent, he couldn't be rightfully compared to Magic Johnson or Larry Bird until he had led the Chicago Bulls to at least one NBA championship.

Mario seemed to take the view that he had established himself as the heir apparent, but that Gretzky was still The One. "I thought it was about time that I started to show my stuff. It all started, really, at the Canada Cup, playing with Wayne. I learned a lot from him. In my opinion, he's still the best player in the world. He had an injury this year and I took advantage of it."

9

Peak Performance

Although hockey news doesn't usually even make it to the sports section during the summer months, Wayne Gretzky was a front-page story twice during the summer of 1989. The first time was in July, when he married Hollywood actress Janet Jones. Then, in August, shock waves traveled through the NHL when it was announced that Gretzky had been traded from the Edmonton Oilers to the Los Angeles Kings. The entire hockey world was stunned by the fact that the player who held most of the NHL's significant scoring records had been traded. But Canadians in particular were shocked to discover that the player they thought of as a national treasure was going to be playing south of the border.

When Mario heard the news, it occurred to him that he would have an easier path to the scoring title, now that Gretzky wasn't going to be surrounded with the type of talent that he had played with in Edmonton. But Mario was more interested in the changes in Pittsburgh, where Tony Esposito had taken over as general manager and hired Gene Ubriaco to coach the Pens.

Esposito, a former NHL netminder, made a significant early-season swap with the Buffalo Sabres that brought goalie Tom Barrasso to Pittsburgh. Barrasso, who had won the Calder Trophy as Rookie of the Year as well as the Vezina Trophy as the league's best goaltender for his play in the 1983–84 season, gave the Pens the All-Star caliber netminder that they would need to make a serious run at a Stanley Cup championship.

But the major story in Pittsburgh was being written, as usual, by the Magnificent One. Mario began the season by racking up 41 points in his first twelve games, a record-setting pace which included an eight-point outburst against the St. Louis Blues. And he didn't stop lighting up NHL scoreboards until the last horn of the season had been blown.

At times, as in a game against the Vancouver Canucks, Mario skated so smoothly and handled the puck so adroitly, it seemed as if he were unstoppable. "They were literally falling at his feet, one after another," recalled former teammate Randy Cunneyworth. "I froze that picture: three guys behind Mario on the ice, in a heap. I'll never forget it. He ended up behind the net and just reached around and stuffed the puck in. I was on the bench and just started laughing."

Before the season had reached the midway point, Mario had already scored 100 points, cracking the century mark faster than anyone, excepting Gretzky, ever had.

Mario brought 1988 to a memorable close when he celebrated New Year's Eve by torching the New Jersey Devils for eight points, and joined Gretzky as the only other player to post two eight-point games in one season.

Mario added a unique touch to that historic game by becoming the first and only player in NHL history to score a goal from every possible formation. He clicked when the teams were at even strength. He lit the red light when the Pens were on a power play, and when they were shorthanded. Mario added his fourth goal on a rare penalty shot, and then he closed out the scoring with an empty-net goal that secured a hard-fought 8–6 victory for the Pens.

"Some of the things he did out there were amazing, even when he didn't score," marveled former teammate Rob Brown. "He put the puck through his legs and made some dazzling twirls. It was a classic example of the best hockey player in the world."

Mario's performance now went beyond shooting the puck and scoring goals. He was playing all over the rink and putting out the type of effort that finally won the approval of hockey traditionalist and Hall of Famer, Gordie Howe. "He's doing a heck of a lot better than he's done before," said Howe, a tough, two-way player who had set most of the NHL's career scoring standards before the Great Gretzky came along and started rewriting the record book. "Before he started to work harder, I used to see him play a five-minute hockey game sometimes," said Howe, who could now applaud Mario's attitude as well as his ability.

Although Mario's production slipped somewhat in February, he bounced right back in March and finished the season the way he had started it, with a scoring surge in which he notched thirteen goals in only six games. That barrage of goals gave Mario a league-high 85 for the season. Only Gretzky, who had bagged 92 during the 1981–82 season and 87 in the 1983–84 campaign, had ever scored more.

Included in Mario's total was an NHL-record 13 short-handed scores, and a league-leading 31 power play goals which helped the Pens set an NHL record with 119 power play scores.

Mario also tied Gretzky for the league lead in assists with 114, and joined the Great One—who had done it for the ninth time—as the only two players to dish out 100 or more assists in a single season.

Although Mario was disappointed that he just missed reaching the 200-point threshold that only Gretzky had ever crossed, his 199 points, a career-high, was the fifth highest total ever recorded in the NHL, and earned him his second consecutive Art Ross Trophy by a comfortable 31-point margin over Gretzky.

Mario was shocked and angered when it was announced that Gretzky had outpolled him in the voting for the Hart Trophy. While there was no arguing with the fact that Gretzky had turned a dormant Kings team into a playoff contender, Mario had done much the same thing in Pittsburgh, and he had scored 31 more goals than Gretzky. "In the past, it's always gone to the best player, the top scorer," said Mario, with a fair degree of accuracy. "I don't know why it should change now."

Mario may have been correct in thinking that his second-place finish had more to do with what went on off the ice than what occurred on it. While Gretzky, with his friendly disposition and outgoing personality, had always cooperated with the media, Mario, who was more introverted and less free with his time, was not popular with reporters. "I don't go out of my way to be nice to reporters. That's just the way I am."

But of greater importance than individual awards and popularity contests was the indisputable fact that at long last Mario's superlative performance had propelled the Penguins to a second-place finish in the Patrick Division and, after four frustrating years of coming up empty, a long-sought spot in the playoffs.

Mario didn't set off any offensive fireworks in the opening round of the playoffs, but the Pens still managed to sweep the Rangers in four straight.

Next in line for Pittsburgh were the Philadelphia Flyers, who proved to be a much tougher test of how far the Pens had come as a team. The cross-state rivals split the first four games while Mario stayed mired in a mild slump that saw him total only ten points in his first eight playoff games.

In the pivotal fifth game, though, Mario exploded like a Roman candle, racking up another eight-point game, and leading the Pens to a wild 10–7 win.

Mario, who scored four of his five goals in the first period, tied five single-game playoff scoring records and made other All-Stars talk like fans. "I've seen a lot of miraculous things in my career," marveled Paul Coffey, who had played with Gretzky for seven seasons prior to joining Pittsburgh. "But I still find myself shaking my head at some of the things that Mario does."

But after gorging himself in Game Five, Mario slept like a stuffed python, as he added only one more point while the Pens were losing the final two games of the series.

Although Mario was disappointed in his lack of scoring punch and the team's elimination from the playoffs, he knew that the Penguins were still a couple of key players away from realistically competing for a Stanley Cup championship. "Hopefully, we can regroup next year and go to the finals. I know I'll drink from that Cup one day. I just know it."

10

Great Expectations

Mario approached the 1989–90 season with great expectations for himself and the team. After his breakout season of 1988–89, Mario believed that he was ready to make a run at Gretzky's single-season records for goals (92), and points (215). And now that the Penguins had finally gotten over the hump and entered into the playoff picture, Mario was hoping that they were about to take an even bigger step.

But the Pens stumbled to a 3–7–2 start, and Mario was so off his game and feeling so sluggish that he went to a doctor for a checkup. "I don't have the jump I had last year," he explained. "I don't have my legs."

The low point in this period came in the twelfth game of the new season when the LA Kings invaded the Igloo on Halloween and spooked the Pens, 8–4. While Gretzky dominated the game with a hat trick and three assists, Mario was limited to two assists. Once again, the Pens were dwelling in their divisional cellar while Mario was looking up at Gretzky in the race for the Art Ross Trophy.

Ironically, though, that game turned out to be a real trick-and-treat night, because it also marked the start of a major consecutive-game scoring streak by Mario. And as soon as Mario caught fire, the Pens started to heat up and climb toward the top of the Patrick Division standings.

In the midst of this run, both general manager Tony Esposito and coach Gene Ubriaco were fired and replaced by one man, Craig Patrick. It was a move that Mario and most of the other players applauded. Patrick brought a new style and a clear vision of what it took to win the Stanley Cup. Like most coaches in team sports, Patrick believed in the old cliché that while the offense earns headlines, it's a team's defense that wins championships. If anyone thought that Mario would have a problem with Patrick's philosophy, they were totally disappointed. "It's been proven that it takes a good defense to win a Stanley Cup," said Mario. "That's what we need to do here in Pittsburgh."

Despite the Pens' new emphasis on defense, Mario kept putting points up on the scoreboard, and rode a 35-game scoring streak into the 1990 All-Star Game, played on January 21st at the Igloo.

Mario gave the hometown fans exactly what they wanted by exploding for a first-period hat trick on his way to a four-goal night and his third All-Star Game MVP award. "It was special when I stepped on the ice," said Mario, whose outburst powered the Wales Conference to a 12–7 shootout win over the Campbell Conference. "I wanted to do something special for the fans in Pittsburgh, and that created a lot of pressure for me. But I was fortunate to get off to a good start, and then the adrenalin really started flowing. I was lucky."

"I could tell that he was pumped up before the game even started," said Gretzky, a member of the losing Campbell squad. "Then he scored the first goal on his first shift and he took his game up a few more notches in a hurry."

But only a few days after that golden game, Mario started to suffer severe pain in his lower back due to a herniated disc. Mario, though, was determined to play through the pain and try to break the 51-game consecutive-game scoring streak record that Gretzky had set during the 1983–84 season.

Mario extended the streak to 41 games with a four-point effort against Edmonton that also catapulted him past Gretzky and into first place in the scoring race.

In order to cut down on the wear and tear on his back, Mario stopped attending practices and limited his ice time to power play opportunities. "I feel I can still go out and help the team. Once I can't do that anymore, then we'll see about getting a little rest."

Mario stretched the streak to 46 games, five games away from Gretzky's record. But that's as far as it went. The chase finally came to an end on February 14th at New York's Madison Square Garden, when the pain became so disabling that Mario couldn't even leave the locker room for the start of the third period.

The injury was so severe that it sidelined Mario for six weeks, and in his absence the Penguins, with only five wins in twenty-one games, plunged in the Patrick Division standings. Still, with one game left in the regular season, the Pens could have put themselves into the playoffs with a win against the Buffalo Sabres. Although his back wasn't fully healed, Mario decided to suit up and try to provide the spark that would ignite the Pens into postseason play.

But there wasn't going to be a storybook ending to this season. While Mario did his part by firing in a goal and adding an assist, the Pens lost in overtime, 3–2, and closed out the season in fifth place in the Patrick Division.

11

That Championship Feeling

The 1990–91 season couldn't have gotten off to a more pessimistic beginning for Mario and the Penguins.

Mario had hoped to control his back pain with a program of physical therapy, but when it became obvious that the exercises weren't helping, he decided to have an operation that would, hopefully, relieve the relentless and disabling pain.

Mario had the surgery on July 11th, and was up and skating six weeks later. "I feel great, painwise," said Mario. But only a few weeks later, the pain was worse than it had ever been.

The doctors diagnosed the condition as an infection that was unrelated to the disc surgery, which they deemed to have been a success. The new treatment they prescribed called for an extended program of antibiotics that would keep Mario on the shelf until the end of January.

The infection caused Mario to miss the first 50 games of the season. Discounting the previous season's finale against the Sabres, Mario had lost the equivalent of an entire season just as he was entering his prime-time years. His medical problems also preyed on Mario's mind, causing him to wonder if he would ever again be able to play the game that he had loved since childhood and that was so central to his being. It made him realize just how fragile life can be, and just how quickly we can lose what we sometimes take for granted. "I see the game a lot differently now. Every time I have a chance to play the game I think I'll approach it a lot differently. It makes you think a lot and realize how lucky you are."

Mario's return to the ice came on January 26th against the

Quebec Nordiques. Despite the long layoff and the accumulated rust, Mario made an immediate contribution by dishing out three assists that helped the visiting Pens achieve a 6–5 win.

"It was special to play this first match in Quebec, in front of my family and several friends. For the past week or so, I set this game as my objective, but nothing could be confirmed because from one day to the next we didn't know how I'd react to the training sessions."

Mario also acknowledged that he was concerned about how his back would react to a hit. "Especially in the first period, I was thinking about being checked." But the fear left Mario after he survived a check by Nordiques forward Paul Gillis that dropped him to the ice. "After that, I just played and didn't have anything on my mind."

While Mario had been on the mend, Craig Patrick had made a lot of moves to upgrade the team, starting with the hiring of Bob Johnson, an easygoing and knowledgeable coach who quickly earned the respect and affection of his players.

Patrick added youth and firepower with the drafting of Jaromir Jagr, an explosive forward who went on to earn a spot on the NHL All-Rookie Team. He also added experience, depth, and scoring punch with the acquisition of two key veterans, right wing Joe Mullen and defenseman Larry Murphy.

Patrick's shrewd moves had put together a team that was able to remain competitive even while Mario had been sidelined. And even after Mario returned and was rounding into shape, scoring 45 points in 26 games, Patrick kept maneuvering. In his final deal of the season, Patrick picked the pockets of the Hartford Whalers by obtaining center Ron Francis and hard-hitting backliner Ulf Samuelsson in a trade that he hoped would supply the missing pieces in the Penguins' quest for a Stanley Cup championship.

The Penguins took an important step toward the Cup by taking the top spot in the Patrick Division, their first divisional title in the twenty-four-year history of the franchise.

But it looked as though their trip would be short-lived when they fell behind the Devils, three games to two, and also lost the services of Tom Barrasso for the remainder of the series. Although Ron Francis fired off a game-winning goal in Game Six to tie the series 3–3, the Pens' chances still seemed bleak when back spasms prevented Mario from suiting up for the seventh game. But the plucky Pens pulled together and banged out a 4–2 win that advanced them to a divisional finals matchup against the Washington Capitals.

Even with Mario back in the lineup, the Pens dropped the opening game to the Caps, but they bounced back and swept the next four games with left wing Kevin Stevens stepping up and swatting home three game-winning goals. "It's been a long time, for myself and a lot of other players in Pittsburgh," said Mario, with a big smile on his face. "It was important for our team to finally get over the hurdle and show our fans we could get out of the Patrick Division."

The Pens, though, proceeded to put themselves into another perilous position when they dropped the first two games of the conference finals to the Bruins in the cramped confines of the Boston Garden. Not only were they down 2–0, but they were also missing Paul Coffey, who was sidelined for the series with a broken jaw.

But home cooking and a tough defense gave the Pens back-to-back 4–1 wins at the Igloo, and then they returned to Boston and battered the Bruins 7–1 to take a 3–2 lead in the series. Although Mario hadn't supplied his usual quota of offensive fireworks, his defensive play had helped to turn the series around. "He's coming back and stripping guys," noted teammate Mark Recchi. "You can see the determination on his face. He really wants to win."

The Pens put the Bruins away by winning Game Six at the

Igloo, 5–3. As if to symbolize how Pittsburgh had been transformed into a team that was no longer solely dependent on one superstar, five different players scored the goals that lifted the Penguins into their first Stanley Cup Finals. Somehow, though, it was absolutely fitting that Mario was the one to score the empty-netter that secured the big win.

The only other team still standing was the surprising Minnesota North Stars, a team that had made it into the playoffs on a pass after finishing the regular season with a 27–39–14 record, the sixteenth worst record out of the twenty-one teams that were in the NHL at the time.

But the North Stars had gotten hot at exactly the right time and knocked off three teams that had finished above them in the standings. They didn't show any great respect for the Penguins, either, as they opened the finals round by beating Pittsburgh at the Igloo, 5–4.

Mario, meanwhile, after waiting seven years to get on this stage, flubbed his lines. "I played badly. I had no energy. No legs." But Mario made up for his poor play with a picture-perfect goal in Game Two which shifted the momentum of the contest toward the Pens and sent them on their way to a 4–1 win.

Mario was sidelined for Game Three by back spasms so severe that he couldn't tie the laces on his skates. The resourceful North Stars took advantage of Mario's absence to skate off with a 3–1 home ice win that gave them a 2–1 lead in the series.

Fortunately for Mario and the Pens, the spasms vanished as suddenly as they had appeared, and Mario was able to return to the lineup and lead the Penguins to three straight wins, including an 8–0 blowout in the Game Six finale that earned the team its first Stanley Cup championship.

Mario, who had four points in the series clincher, led all playoff scorers with 44 points in 16 games, only three shy of the NHL record of 47 that Gretzky had set in 18 games in 1985.

"It seemed like anything that was within twenty feet, he reached," said the North Star's Dave Gagner. "When somebody that big and that good wants to win that badly, there isn't much you can do to stop him."

"You dream of this, but it's even better in real life than it is in your dreams," declared Mario, who capped seven years of individual brilliance, frustration, and career-threatening injuries by winning the Conn Smythe Trophy as the MVP of the playoffs. "This means everything to me. To be part of a championship team after the back problems and the surgery and infections—this is the ultimate dream."

"Dominating a Stanley Cup victory was the one thing left for Mario to achieve in establishing himself as one of the truly great players in the history of hockey," said coach Bob Johnson. "If there were any questions left, I think he's supplied the answers."

12

Back-to-Back

If the Penguins imagined that life as Stanley Cup champions was going to be as easy as a walk down the Yellow Brick Road, they quickly found out otherwise.

Before the team had even reassembled for the start of training camp, they discovered that their coach, Bob Johnson, had been stricken with a fatal disease. The news stunned and saddened the team. "What he's done for this city and this hockey club in one year is pretty incredible," said Mario. "Nobody thought we'd win the Cup, but with Bob Johnson, anything is possible."

Johnson was replaced behind the bench, but not in the affections of the team, by Scotty Bowman, a coach who had already been enshrined in the Hockey Hall of Fame. Bowman was undeniably strong on tactics, but he lacked Johnson's warmth and player communication skills. "Bob really cared about you on and off the ice," noted right wing Mark Recchi. "He had a way of raising the level of your play by always saying something positive. With Scotty Bowman, you're lucky if you get a 'hi' out of him. It's different."

Another problem confronting the team at the outset involved salary disputes between the owner and some top players, including the left wing on Mario's line, Kevin Stevens. Stevens, one of the rising stars in the game, had become a free agent and had received a long-term, big-bucks offer from the Boston Bruins.

Although Mario usually preferred to remain in the background, he was so concerned about the possible breakup of a championship team that he issued a public challenge to the owner through the press. "I guess we're going to find out if the Penguins want to win another Stanley Cup. If they do, they have to sign Kevin."

The Penguins quickly matched the Bruins' offer to Stevens and also signed Ron Francis and Ulf Samuelsson to long-term deals. Back on the ice, however, the team wasn't faring so well. During the first half of the 1991–92 season, the Penguins played more like competent contenders than reigning champions. While they were humming along offensively, there were major problems with the defense. With Mario leading the league in scoring and Kevin Stevens right behind him, the Penguins had the most potent offense in the NHL. On the flip side, however, they had one of the leakiest defenses, and they were giving up goals almost as quickly as they scored them.

Given that imbalance, it wasn't surprising that the Pens reached the midpoint of the season in the middle of the pack in the Patrick Division. And while they weren't anywhere close to being the dominating team that they had hoped to be, they still seemed like a sure bet to be in the postseason picture.

In January, though, Mario suffered a relapse of the back spasms, which caused him to miss games, and the Pens began to slide down in the standings. Mario had hoped that he'd be able to play the rest of his career in a pain-free state, but this latest episode convinced him otherwise. "Every move I make, I have to be careful. The awareness that my hockey career can end at any time is always there."

Mario's love of the game is strong, but his willingness to play through excruciating pain and still perform at such an extraordinary level, is mind-boggling. "I've been in this business for twelve years and I can't believe what he goes through, just to play this game," said the Pens' strength and conditioning coach, John Welday, one of the three members of the Pittsburgh training staff who spend a half hour before each game trying to get Mario ready to skate. "We all do what we can to try to ease his pain and help him loosen up, but he's the one who has to go and play. He's not a big talker, but the rest of the guys see what he goes through. That's why he wears the captain's 'C' on his chest."

What most people don't realize is that Mario was able to stay at the front of the pack even though the pain forced him to miss about three of every four practices. "I don't know how he does it," said an admiring Kevin Stevens, who has blossomed into the best left wing in the NHL. "How do you keep your hands sharp? Your legs? If I miss a day or two of practice, it takes me a week to get it back.

"Mario's so scary out there. It's ridiculous how far ahead of everyone else he is. He is the best player in the world—by far. If you're sitting in the stands and you're not amazed, you don't deserve to be sitting in the stands."

In February, after the defense hadn't shown any signs of improvement, Craig Patrick initiated a bold, three-team trade that sent All-Star defenseman Paul Coffey to the LA Kings, and Mark Recchi, a hard-nosed, high-scoring right wing, to the Philadelphia Flyers. In return, the Pens received a stay-at-home defenseman, Kjell Samuelsson, and Rich Tocchet, a strong two-way winger.

While some people suggested that the swaps had been motivated by a desire to trim the payroll of an overpaid, underachieving team, Patrick defended the three-cornered trade. "We moved two very offensive players for some people who were bigger, stronger, and maybe more defensive-minded that what we gave up. Plus, we felt Tocchet could give us a lot of the offense that we might be giving up, and he could also give us a physical presence on the ice and better defense."

Despite Patrick's best-laid plans, the trade didn't slow the slide of the Pens, who woke up on the morning of March 3rd as a fourth-place team, only one game above .500, just three points ahead of the fifth-place Islanders, and a mere five points ahead of the last-place Flyers.

Contributing to the Pens' downfall was a season-long rift between Bowman and the players. With the season hanging in the balance, Patrick met with the team to remind them that they had overcome a lot of adversity during the season and that they could pull together again and defend their hard-won championship. "I told them to look beyond the exterior and try to feed off Bowman's immense knowledge and experience. It wasn't like we just brought in some flunky off the street and asked him to coach; Scotty Bowman won five Stanley Cup titles as the coach of the Montreal Canadiens."

Patrick had sounded the alarm and the players, with only seventeen games left to salvage their season, responded to the wake-up call by closing out the season with an 11–5–1 record that moved them back into third place and into position to make a run at a second Stanley Cup.

The main man in the stretch run was Super Mario, who compiled a 14-game scoring streak in which he totaled 37 points and earned NHL Player of the Month honors for March.

Although he'd been able to suit up for only 64 games, Mario's finishing kick gave him a league-high total of 131 points, eight points ahead of runner-up Kevin Stevens, who had played in all 80 games, and ten points better than Wayne Gretzky, who had played in 74 contests.

In picking up his third Art Ross Trophy in five years, Mario had become one of only eight players in NHL history to win as many as three scoring titles. Even more impressively, Mario had become the first player since Hall of Famer Bernie "Boom Boom" Geoffrion to win a scoring title while playing in as few as 64 games. What made Mario's achievement more significant than the Boomer's, however, was that Geoffrion had won his title in the 1960–61 season, when a schedule was 70 games. So Geoffrion only had to spot the rest of the league six games whereas Mario had to overcome a sixteen-game handicap to capture his scoring title.

Mario also hit a number of milestones during the season, including his 400th career goal on March 14th, against the Toronto Maple Leafs; his 600th career assist on March 26th, versus the Vancouver Canucks; and his 1000th career point on March 22nd, against the Detroit Red Wings. Mario reached the 1000-point level in 513 games, faster than any other player in NHL history, excepting Gretzky, who turned the trick in 424 contests.

The strong stretch run had warmed Mario and his teammates for the trial-by-fire of the playoffs. Individual records and rewards are satisfying, but the most enduring rewards for athletes in team sports are team championships. Plain and simple, Mario and Company intended to hold on to Lord Stanley's silver until some other team was strong enough to pull it out of their grasp.

Which is exactly what the Washington Capitals came within one game of achieving in the opening round of the playoffs. The Caps, who had finished with the second best record in the NHL, ambushed the Pens in Game One, while Mario sat on the sidelines with a sore shoulder. Although Mario returned to action for the second game, the results were exactly the same and the Pens' grasp of the Cup seemed very slippery. In the third game, though, Super Mario rose to the occasion by setting up the Pens' first three goals and scoring the last three himself to power the Pens to a 6–4 win. But Mario's great game seemed beside the point after the Caps had stormed back to capture the next contest, 7–2, and take a commanding 3–1 lead in the series.

Just when it appeared that the Pens were about to be deposed, Mario went to Bowman with a series-saving suggestion. As Washington coach Terry Murray would later acknowledge, "I think the changes the Penguins made against us turned the series around."

Mario's idea was to slow down the Caps' offense by sending only one forechecker into the attacking zone, while the other four Pens would retreat into the neutral zone. Using this style of play, reasoned Mario, would prevent the Caps from initiating the quick breakouts that were the backbone of their offense.

The Pens carried out the strategy to near-perfection in Game Four, as they bottled up the Caps and skated off with a 5–2 win. Although the Caps did manage to break out for four goals in the next game, Mario once again took matters into his own hands with a five-point explosion, including the game-winning goal, that led the Pens to a come-from-behind 6–4 win and evened the series at 3–3.

The Pens tightened their defense again in the decisive seventh game, and Mario seemed to suck the breath of life right out of the Caps when he turned a Washington power play into a shorthanded goal that sparked the Penguins to a series-clinching 3–1 win, and capped their spine-tingling comeback.

"We were beaten by one man," declared Washington coach, Terry Murray. "Number 66. Lemieux. Right now, he's the best player in the NHL."

When David Poile, the Caps' general manager, asked Jack Ferreira, his counterpart with the San Jose Sharks, what mistakes his team had made in letting the Pens pull out the series, Ferreira had a short and simple response. "You didn't do anything wrong. Mario just decided to take over."

The next challenge for the Penguins was the New York Rangers, the team that had finished with the best overall record in the league, 19 points ahead of Pittsburgh. But the Pens, who had dropped five of their seven regular season meetings with the Rangers, rode Mario's play-making to a 4–2 win in the series opener. "Nobody in the world is playing

70

better than Mario," declared Kevin Stevens, who had scored one of the Pens' goals after a picture-perfect setup from Mario. "He's the guy they have to key on, and that opens it up for the rest of us."

The Rangers realized that they had to stop the Big Guy; they just didn't know how to do it. "Throw a net over him," suggested Mike Gartner, the Rangers' high-scoring right wing. "Better yet, maybe we should shoot him."

While Gartner was obviously joking, the Rangers did take Mario out of the series in the following game when Adam Graves, wielding his stick like an axe, delivered a two-handed slash with such ferocity that it broke Mario's left wrist.

To many observers, this was another shocking example of the brutality that is allowed to flourish in the NHL. Although Graves eventually received a four-game suspension, the penalty was much less severe than the crime. As Ron Francis pointed out, "Graves is lost to the Rangers for four games, but we've lost Mario for longer than that. The league has to start taking a tougher stance. The league has been too lenient, and that's why things have reached this stage."

Hockey will be a much better sport if the powers-that-be ever realize that hockey sticks should only be allowed to be used as a skilled tool and not as a blunt weapon. Just imagine what would have happened to, say, Paul Molitor, if during the World Series he went to the pitcher's mound and used his bat to slash the wrist of, say, Mitch Williams.

A league that condones fighting and stick-wielding attacks by handing out minimun penalties not only risks losing its stars to brutish attacks, but also diminishes the artistry of the game by reserving roster spots for bullies that should be filled by more skilled players. A league that condones fighting and stick-wielding is, simply, an affront to all civilized people.

Although Graves, who had no prior history of being a

hockey goon, denied that he was trying to hurt Mario, the suspicion remains that the Ranger coach at the time, Roger Neilson, had put a bounty out on Mario. Neilson did nothing to disturb those dark thoughts when he blithely told reporters, "It's great not having to worry about Lemieux."

The Rangers no longer had to concern themselves with Joe Mullen, either, since he had gone down and out of the playoffs with a knee injury. With two of their three top goal-scorers on the shelf, it looked as though the Pens' drive to a second Stanley Cup was about to come to a screeching halt.

But instead of breaking, the tough and resilient Penguins rolled right over the Rangers, four games to two. Tom Barrasso became nearly unpassable in goal, while Larry Murphy, Kevin Stevens, Jaromir Jagr, and especially Ron Francis, who scored ten points over the final four games, kept the Pens' offense in overdrive. "I'm not Mario or Joe Mullen," said Francis, with unfeigned modesty. "I can't replace them. But I felt I had to do something with them gone."

"I think the Rangers made a tactical error by playing cheap early in the series," declared Rick Tocchet. "They underestimated the dedication that made this a championship team. They underestimated the desire that this team has to win it all again."

The next roadblock for the Pens was the Boston Bruins, who had captured the Adams Division title with a four-game sweep over the Montreal Canadiens. But the Lemieux-less Penguins stopped the streaking Bruins with a victory in the first game. And then Mario, with a cast on his wrist, and playing as if he hadn't missed a shift, made a triumphant two-goal, three-point return to spark the Pens to a 5–2 win. Although Mario's wrist hadn't healed enough to go to his backhand, veteran center Bryan Trottier knew his teammate's worth. "Mario playing at fifty percent is better than any of us playing at one hundred percent."

Buoyed by Mario's return, the Pens went on to sweep the

Bruins, while Mario earned the admiration of everyone who had seen him play. "He's the best player in the league," declared Boston's All-Star defenseman, Ray Bourque. "One of the greatest, if not the greatest, ever to play the game. You can see Mario wants a shot at winning another Stanley Cup title, and he doesn't plan on being denied."

The only obstacle that now remained in the Pens' path was the Campbell Conference champion Chicago Blackhawks, who rode a playoff-record 11-game winning streak into the finals. The tough-checking team from the Windy City was playing airtight defense, backed by red-hot goalie Ed Belfour, who had surrendered only 15 goals while compiling a 12–1 record in the playoffs. It seemed as though the irresistable force was about to butt up against the immovable object.

But Ray Bourque was right: Mario was not about to be denied. In Game One, he rallied the Pens from a three-goal deficit and scored the game-winner with only 13 clicks left on the clock. Mario came right back with another pair of goals to lead the Pens to a 3–1 win in the second game. The Pens out-defensed Chicago, 1–0, in the third game, and then they got out their brooms and outscored them 6–5 to finish off the sweep and earn their second consecutive Stanley Cup championship.

Despite missing six games, Mario still led all playoff scorers with 34 points, and tied a playoff record with five game-winning goals. That spectacular string of performances earned Super Mario a second consecutive Conn Smythe Trophy as the MVP of the playoffs, the first repeat winner since Flyer goalie Bernie Parent accomplished the feat in 1974 and 1975.

"The Penguins *are* Mario Lemieux," announced Mike Keenan, Chicago's coach. "They have a lot of great players, but a player like Mario is how you win Stanley Cups."

13

Most Remarkable

The 1992–93 season stands as the most remarkable season in Mario's magnificent career. It is, in fact, one of the most remarkable seasons that any athlete has ever produced.

After signing a seven-year, forty-two-million-dollar contract on October 5th, which made him the highest paid player in hockey history, Mario went out and immediately began earning all that money by stringing together a twelve-game goal-scoring streak, which earned him two consecutive NHL Player of the Week awards as well as NHL Player of the Month honors for October. Mario was playing in one of those amazing "zones" in which it felt as if he were in complete control of the game.

"Everything seems to slow down, and I'm seeing everything on the ice. Everything seems to come easy. Every time I get the puck I see the whole ice; who is open, who is not. It doesn't happen very often, but if I'm playing really well, I can go four or five games like that. When I'm on the ice, it feels natural. But when I look at the replay, sometimes even I'm amazed."

Although Mario's consecutive-game goal-scoring streak finally came to an end, he continued to pile up points at a record-threatening pace. "It's almost scary," said NHL veteran Dave Poulin. "It looks like he's toying with you, like he can turn it on at any moment. That's how good he is."

As 1992 drew to a close, Mario capped off the year, as he had in 1988, with a gala New Year's Eve celebration. Mario came into the game, his 37th of the season, needing only one point to join the century club for the eighth time in his career, and he didn't waste too much time in reaching the milestone.

With just over three minutes left in the opening period, and the Pens down a man, Mario gathered in a Ron Francis pass near the red line. Then he used his strength to keep muscling his way around Toronto Maple Leaf defenseman Dmitri Mironov until he was close enough to roll the puck past goalie Grant Fuhr for his 37th goal of the season.

"I lost control of the puck a couple of times and Mironov got a whack at it. I got it back on my forehand and was able to put it in," said Mario, who later added an assist to his scoring total. "Once he has the puck," explained Mironov, "it's too late."

Mario's 37 goals and 64 assists in 37 games tied him for the fourth-fastest 100 points from the beginning of an NHL season. Wayne Gretzky did it in 34 games in 1983–84 and in 35 games the following season, while Mario turned the trick in 36 games in 1988–89. No other player in NHL history has ever scored 100 points from the start of a season in fewer than forty games.

Mario was soaring through life like a high-flying bird. He was pain-free and playing at the top of his game as the leader of the best team in hockey. "Right now," acknowledged Mario, "I'm at my peak."

"He's the most dominant hockey player the game has ever seen," raved Boston general manager, Harry Sinden, who had seen most of the game's fabled players and had coached Bobby Orr, the Hall of Fame defenseman whose offensive skills had revolutionized the sport.

Although 1992 had ended on such a high note, Mario was looking forward to even better times to come, including a third consecutive Stanley Cup championship and a June wedding to his long-time girlfriend, Nathalie Asselin. Life was not only good, it seemed golden. But within two short weeks, it all seemed to turn to straw.

On Friday, January 15, 1993, Mario held a news conference to tell the world what he had known since the previous Monday, that he had Hodgkin's disease, a form of cancer. Although the doctor had told Mario that they had caught the disease at an early stage so that he had a ninety to ninety-five percent chance for a full recovery, Mario took the news badly.

"I could hardly drive because of the tears," said Mario. "That first day was a tough day for me. It's scary every time you hear the word 'cancer'."

What made the diagnosis even more frightening for Mario was the fact that two of his uncles had died of cancer and a young cousin had actually died from Hodgkin's.

By the day of the press conference, though, Mario had started to come to terms with the illness and his prospects for recovery. "I'm a positive person by nature and that's not going to change in the future even though I have Hodgkin's. That's not going to change my life and the way I live it. Certainly it's going to make it tougher for the next couple of months but that's life sometimes . . . Sometimes in life you have to go through some tough periods and certainly I haven't been too fortunate the last few years with my back surgery, back infection, recurrence of back problems, and my hand broken in the playoffs last year. But it's a tough sport and sometimes you have to go through some injuries and climb the mountain. This is certainly another mountain that I have to climb."

Before the press conference, Mario had gone to see his shocked and worried teammates. "I walked in the room and everybody was silent. That's not our team. Kevin Stevens talks all the time and Ulfy Samuellson is always yapping."

"It just seems everything just keeps coming down on him," said linemate Kevin Stevens. But Tom Barrasso, whose daughter had survived a bout with childhood leukemia just two years earlier, was sure that Mario would get well and come back, just as he always had. "People who don't understand the disease will make it sound a lot worse than his particular prognosis is. He has been through traumatic injuries, traumatic treatments before and this is no different."

Before Mario could begin radiation treatments to combat the cancer, he had to be placed on antibiotics for two weeks to cure another, more minor illness. Then Mario began a month of radiation therapy during which he was blasted with three doses of X rays for a few minutes each morning, five days a week. The treatments weren't physically painful but they were a daily and inescapable reminder of how precious life is.

Mario began skating with the Penguins in February and on March 2nd, after he had had his last radiation treatment, Mario returned to action in a game against the Flyers at the Spectrum. As usual, Mario was the last player to skate out on the ice, but as soon as he came into view, he received a standing ovation from the normally hostile Philly fans. Mario acknowledged the emotional outpouring with a tip of his stick and then, as though he had never been away, went on to score one goal and set up another. Amazing! Although the Penguins lost the game, 5–4, the score, in this case, was completely beside the point. "It feels great that I can get back to doing what I love best: playing hockey," said Mario.

And players all around the league welcomed Mario's return. "We're all assuming that he's going to start off where he left off," said Detroit center Steve Yzerman. "He's the best player in the game, the Number One marquee player, and for sentimental reasons, I want him to be healthy as well."

But as happy as everyone was that Mario was back, he knew that he wasn't going to receive any special treatment. "If the hit's there, I'll take it," said the Islander's Rich Pilon. "But he's a very hard player to hit. You can't take a run at him because he'll take you out of position and burn you. He's like a ballerina."

The Pens also dropped their next game, but then Mario went off on an incredible 16-game, 51-point scoring binge and the team reeled off an NHL-record 17-game winning streak before they ended the season with a 6–6 tie against the Devils.

"Mario came back from his illness and got his game back to a high level right away," said defenseman Larry Murphy. "The other players could see that and everyone else has elevated their game since then."

"When Mario's out there," added Kevin Stevens, "we feel we can win every time out."

During Mario's spectacular 51-point scoring streak, he piled up 27 goals and 24 assists, including a five-goal barrage in the Pens' record-setting sixteenth straight win against the New York Rangers in Madison Square Garden.

The performance was so transcendent that the Rangers rose and gave Mario a standing ovation. Mario's sensational scoring surge also allowed him to overtake Pat LaFontaine and win his fourth Art Ross Trophy by a twelve goal margin, despite the fact that Mario had missed 24 contests and LaFontaine had played in all 84 games.

"What Mario is doing now is scary," declared Kevin Stevens. "You know how a game looks when you sit high above and watch it? Mario seems like he's watching the game above everyone else.

"We've all seen him play the last few years and he never ceases to amaze us. But this one takes everything. What he's done here, I've never seen in any sport. It's beyond hockey."

The Penguins went into the playoffs as a supremely confident hockey team. They were the two-time defending Stanley Cup champions and their late-season surge had earned the President's Trophy for having the best overall record in the NHL. They had finished the season with 119 points, a full 26 points better than the Caps, their closest pursuer in the Patrick Division, and 10 points ahead of the Boston Bruins, who had finished with the second best overall record. "This is definitely the best team I've ever played with," declared Mario. "We have three lines that can score a lot of goals, a lot of guys who can put the puck in the net. It's pretty tough to find guys who can score thirty, forty, fifty goals, but we have them on every line. We certainly won't be satisfied with anything less than the Stanley Cup."

Most of the media as well as competing coaches made it seem as if the Pens were invincible. "If they play to their potential and Mario plays all the games, I don't think they can be beaten," said TV analyst and former NHL goalie, John Davidson.

"The margin of error is almost nil against them," added Montreal coach, Jacques Demers. "They know they can win every game they play. They are the greatest team in hockey right now."

The Penguins opened defense of their title according to script with Mario scoring four points and leading the Pens past the Devils, 6–3. Afterwards, Devils center Dave Barr sounded as if he were trying to convince himself as well as answer reporters' questions about a possible sweep when he said, "It's not like they won 84 games in a row. I mean, they *can* lose."

Barr might have had second thoughts after the Pens torched the Devils, 7–0, for their thirteenth consecutive play-off win, breaking the record of twelve straight that had been set by the Gretzky-led Edmonton Oiler teams of 1984 and 1985.

The Pens also took Game Three, 4–3, with Mario leading them back from a two-goal third period deficit. And after the Devils avoided a sweep with a face-saving win in Game Four, the Pens put them out of their misery with a 5–3 win. As the teams exchanged the traditional series-ending handshakes,

Devils defensman Alexsei Kasatorov expressed the ultimate respect for Mario when he asked for the Magnificent One's stick. "He's the best in the world," said Kasatorov, showing off the lumber that Mario had given him.

Next up were the New York Islanders, a team the Pens had outdistanced by 32 points in the regular season. And the Isles would have to play the series without their leading scorer, Pierre Turgeon, who had been put out of commission by a blatant cheap shot delivered by Dale Hunter after Turgeon had already scored the series-winning goal against the Washington Capitals.

But two minutes into the first game, Mario had to leave the ice when back spasms made it impossible for him to play and the Islanders skated off with a 3–2 win. "When Lemieux skated off, the guys on the bench were saying, 'Hey, we've got a real chance to win this game,' " said Steve Thomas of the Islanders.

Right wing Rick Tocchet knew that without Mario, the Pens were without the player that made their engine hum. "We don't have anyone who can make the passes Mario makes. With Mario out, maybe we have to take more shots and forget the pretty plays." But Tom Barrasso tried to look at the positive side. "Playing without Mario is nothing new to us. We've adjusted before and we have to adjust again."

Then Barrasso went out and backed up his brave words by shutting out the Islanders, 3–0. Mario was able to play only sparingly in the next two games, which the team split, and the series stayed even at 2–2. "It's really frustrating to sit upstairs and watch the team play," explained Mario. "It's not a question of playing through pain. When it gets that bad, I just can't do anything. I can't even bend over or move my body. I just have to stay still and wait for the pain to go away."

The pain went away for Game Five, and Mario scored three points, including a tone-setting goal nineteen seconds into the first period, that carried the Penguins to a 6–3 win. "He has ice water in his veins," said Scotty Bowman. "Under tremendous pressure, under surveillance, he finds a way to get it done."

The Pens now needed only one more win to advance to the conference finals, but they couldn't get it done. With Mario's back causing him to limp through the last two games of the series, the Islanders rallied and pulled off one of the most stunning upsets in hockey history.

The Islanders win served to confirm a statement that Harry Sinden had made the previous year. "I have a great deal of respect for the other players on the Pittsburgh team, but they don't win Stanley Cups without Mario. What I'm saying is, they are better than the rest of us because of Mario."

The elimination put a crushing end to Mario's dreams of the Penguins "three-peating" as Stanley Cup champions. But he did have the consolation of picking up his second and virtually uncontested Hart Trophy as the NHL's MVP, to go along with his Art Ross Trophy as the league's scoring leader. Mario, who led the league with a +55 rating, also picked up his third Lester B. Pearson Award as the best player in the league, and was presented with the Masterton Trophy, which is given to the player who best represents the qualities of perserverance, sportsmanship, and dedication to hockey.

Epilogue

During the summer of 1993, Mario had another operation on his back, and his future in hockey is cloudy. But even if he never plays another game Mario has established himself as one of the all-time great players to ever skate on ice.

He has the highest goals-per-game average in NHL history (.827%) and the second highest assists average (1.21%). Beyond all other records, though, is the amazing consistency that Mario had given the Penguins by never going more than seven games without scoring a goal and never more than two games without posting a point.

And if Mario does come back, try to see him while you still can, because there will never be another one quite like him.

In his book, *Showtime*, New York Knicks coach Pat Riley talked about seeing Magic Johnson on a beach during the off season, when both of them were with the Los Angeles Lakers. As Magic walked away, Riley thought, "And there was this guy walking away from me with a gray T-shirt that was slapping in the breeze. I got a shudder. I thought, 'You know, one day he's gonna be gone forever. He's going to walk right out of my life and the Lakers' lives and the fans' lives and that's going to be it . . .' "

So if there's still time, don't miss the *unique* magic of Mario Lemieux, the best one; or as they say in Quebec, "le Magnifique"—the Magnificent.

Sources

Mario, by Lawrence Martin, Lester Publishing
Mario Lemieux, by Robert Italia, Abodo & Daughters
Mario Lemieux: Wizard With a Puck, Bill Gutman
Sports Illustrated
The Sporting News

To write to Mario Lemieux, address your letter to:

> Mario Lemieux
> c/o The Pittsburgh Penguins
> Civic Arena
> Pittsburg PA 15219

To write to the author, address your letter to:

> Richard J. Brenner
> c/o East End Publishing
> 54 Alexander Drive
> Syosset NY 11791

Please enclose a self-addressed and stamped envelope.

MARIO LEMIEUX

CAREER PLAYING RECORD

SEASON	TEAM	LEAGUE	Regular Season					Playoffs				
			GP	G	A	PTS	PIM	GP	G	A	PTS	PIM
1981–82	Laval	QMJHL	64	30	66	96	22	18	5	9	14	31
1982–83	Laval (b)	QMJHL	66	84	100	184	76	12	14	18	32	18
1983–84	Laval (abcde)	QMJHL	70	133*	149*	282*	92	14	29*	23*	52*	29
1984–85	PITTSBURGH (fg)	NHL	73	43	57	100	54	—	—	—	—	—
1985–86	PITTSBURGH (hi)	NHL	79	48	93	141	43	—	—	—	—	—
1986–87	PITTSBURGH (h)	NHL	63	54	53	107	57	—	—	—	—	—
1987–88	PITTSBURGH (ijkl)	NHL	77	70*	98	168*	92	—	—	—	—	—
1988–89	PITTSBURGH (kl)	NHL	76	85*	114*	199*	100	11	12	7	19	16
1989–90	PITTSBURGH	NHL	59	45	78	123	78	—	—	—	—	—
1990–91	PITTSBURGH (m)	NHL	26	19	26	45	30	23	16	28*	44*	16
1991–92	PITTSBURGH (km)	NHL	64	44	87	131*	94	15	16*	18	34*	2
1992–93	PITTSBURGH (ijkln)	NHL	60	69	91	160	38	11	8	10	18	10
	NHL & PGH TOTALS		577	477	697	1174	586	60	52	63	115	44

* – League-leading figure

a – June 1984 – Drafted by Pittsburg in 1984 Entry Draft. First Penguins pick, first overall, first round.
b – QMJHL Second All-Star Team (1982-83)   c – QMJHL First All-Star Team (1983-84)
d – QMJHL Most Valuable Player (1983-84)
e – Canadian Major Junior Player of the Year (1983-84)
f – Won Calder Memorial Trophy (1984-85)   g – NHL All-Rookie Team (1984-85)
h – NHL Second All-Star Team (1984-85 & 1986-87)
i – Won Lester B. Pearson Award (1985-86 & 1987-88)
j – Won Hart Trophy (1987-88)
k – Won Art Ross Trophy (1987-88, 1988-89 & 1991-92)   m – Won Conn Smythe Trophy (1991 & 1992)
l – NHL First All-Star Team (1987-88 & 1988-89)

You might want to order some of our other exciting sports titles:

BASEBALL SUPERSTARS ALBUM 1993, by Richard J. Brenner. Includes Frank Thomas, Juan Gonzales, Paul Molitor, Roberto Alomar, Barry Larkin, Ryne Sandberg, Fred McGriff and ten more baseball superstars. 48 pages including 16 in full color. ($4.00/5.00 Canada)

FOOTBALL SUPERSTARS ALBUM 1993, by Richard J. Brenner. Includes Troy Aikman, Emmitt Smith, Barry Sanders, Steve Young, Warren Moon, Jerry Rice, Junior Seau and ten more football superstars. 48 pages including 16 in full color. ($4.00/5.00 Canada)

BASKETBALL SUPERSTARS ALBUM 1993, by Richard J. Brenner. Includes Michael Jordan, Magic Johnson, David Robinson, Charles Barkley, John Stockton, Larry Johnson, Horace Grant and ten more basketball superstars. 48 pages including 16 in full color. ($4.00/5.00 Canada)

THE WORLD SERIES, The Great Contests, by Richard J. Brenner. The unique excitement of the World Series is brought to life in seven of the most thrilling contests ever played, including the 1991 and 1992 Series. 160 pages, including 16 action-packed photos. ($3.50/4.50 Canada)

THE COMPLETE SUPER BOWL STORY, Games I-XXVII, by Richard J. Brenner. The most exciting moments in Super Bowl history are brought to life, game by game. 208 pages, including 16 memorable photos. ($3.50/4.50 Canada)

SHAQUILLE O'NEAL*LARRY JOHNSON, by Richard J. Brenner. A dual biography of the two brightest young stars in basketball. 96 pages, 10 pages of photos. ($3.50/4.50 Canada)

BARRY BONDS*ROBERTO ALOMAR, by Bob Woods. A dual biography of two of baseball's best players. 96 pages, 10 pages of photos ($3.50/4.50 Canada)

ISIAH THOMAS*CHARLES BARKLEY, by Jordan Deutsch. A lively look at two NBA superstars. 96 pages, 12 photos. ($2.95/3.75 Canada)

MARIO LEMIEUX, by Richard J. Brenner. An exciting biography of hockey's greatest player. 96 pages, 10 pages of photos ($3.50/4.50 Canada)

BRETT HULL, by M.J. Goldstein. An easy-to-read biography of the top goal scorer in the NHL over the last three seasons. 48 pages. Lots of exciting photos. Complete career stats. ($3.00/4.00 Canada)

MICHAEL JORDAN, by Richard J. Brenner. An easy-to-read, photo-filled biography especially for young readers. 32 pages. ($3.00/4.00 Canada)

WAYNE GRETZKY, by Richard J. Brenner. An easy-to-read, photo-filled biography of hockey's top star. 32 pages. ($3.00/4.00 Canada)

ORDER FORM

Please indicate the number of copies of each title that you are ordering.

_____	BASEBALL SUPERSTARS ALBUM 1993	($4.00/5.00 Canada)
_____	FOOTBALL SUPERSTARS ALBUM 1993	($4.00/5.00 Canada)
_____	BASKETBALL SUPERSTARS ALBUM 1993	($4.00/5.00 Canada)
_____	THE WORLD SERIES	($3.50/4.50 Canada)
_____	THE COMPLETE SUPER BOWL STORY	($3.50/4.50 Canada)
_____	SHAQUILLE O'NEAL*LARRY JOHNSON	($3.50/4.50 Canada)
_____	BARRY BONDS*ROBERTO ALOMAR	($3.50/4.50 Canada)
_____	ISIAH THOMAS*CHARLES BARKLEY	($2.95/3.95 Canada)
_____	MARIO LEMIEUX	($3.50/4.50 Canada)
_____	BRETT HULL	($3.00/4.00 Canada)
_____	MICHAEL JORDAN	($3.00/4.00 Canada)
_____	WAYNE GRETZKY	($3.00/4.00 Canada)

Payment must accompany all orders. *All payments must be in U.S. dollars.*
Postage and handling is $1.35 per book up to a maximum of $6.75. ($1.75 to a
   maximum of $8.75 in Canada.)

TOTAL NUMBER OF BOOKS ORDERED   _____
TOTAL COST OF BOOKS $_____
POSTAGE AND HANDLING $_____
TOTAL COST OF ORDER $_____

Please don't forget to enclose a check or money order in U.S. funds only.
Please make checks payable to: EAST END PUBLISHING, Ltd.

54 Alexander Dr.
Syosset, NY 11791

Discounts are available on orders of 25 or more copies. For details, call:
(516-364-6383).

_____

Please print neatly.

NAME: _____

ADDRESS: _____

CITY: _____ STATE: _____ ZIP CODE: _____

PLEASE ALLOW FOUR WEEKS FOR DELIVERY.

Send to: East End Publishing, Ltd., Dept. SB3, 54 Alexander Drive, Syosset,
   NY 11791 USA.